Abigail Adams

First Lady of the American Revolution

written by Patricia Lakin

illustrated by
Bob Dacey and Debra Bandelin

Ready-to-Read • Aladdin
New York   London   Toronto   Sydney

This book is dedicated to you, a future voter! —P. L.

To Anna, Jennifer, Caroline, and Peter,
with love —B. D. & D. B.

❧

ALADDIN PAPERBACKS

An imprint of Simon & Schuster Children's Publishing Division

1230 Avenue of the Americas, New York, NY 10020

Text copyright © 2006 by Patricia Lakin

Illustrations copyright © 2006 by Bob Dacey and Debra Bandelin

All rights reserved, including the right of reproduction in whole or in part in any form.

READY-TO-READ is a registered trademark of Simon & Schuster, Inc.

ALADDIN PAPERBACKS and colophon are trademarks of Simon & Schuster, Inc.

Designed by Lisa Vega

The text of this book was set in CenturyOldst BT.

Manufactured in the United States of America

First Aladdin Paperbacks edition July 2006

2 4 6 8 10 9 7 5 3 1

Library of Congress Cataloging-in-Publication Data

Lakin, Patricia, 1944–

Abigail Adams : first lady of the American Revolution / by Patricia Lakin ;

illustrated by Bob Dacey and Debra Bandelin.—1st Aladdin Paperbacks ed.

p. cm.—(Ready-to-read stories of famous Americans)

ISBN-13: 978-0-689-87032-3 (pbk.)

ISBN-10: 0-689-87032-9 (pbk.)

ISBN-13: 978-0-689-87033-0 (lib.)

ISBN-10: 0-689-87033-7 (lib.)

1. Adams, Abigail, 1744–1818—Juvenile literature. 2. Presidents' spouses—United States—

Biography—Juvenile literature. 3. United States—History—Revolution, 1775–1783—

Juvenile literature. I. Dacey, Bob, ill. II. Bandelin, Debra, ill. III. Title. IV. Series.

E322.1.A38L35 2006

973.4'4'092—dc22

2005007955

CHAPTER 1
ABIGAIL'S EARLY YEARS

Abigail Adams lived at a time in America when women were expected to be wives and mothers—nothing more. But Abigail *was* far more! She helped shape the early history of the United States, influenced two of our nation's presidents, managed the family farm almost single-handedly, and became a clever businesswoman.

Abigail was the second child of Reverend William and Elizabeth Smith. She was born on November 11, 1744. The Smith family lived in a small cottage in Weymouth, Massachusetts, one of the thirteen British colonies that would soon become the United States of America.

Colonial girls did not attend school. Their mothers taught them only what they needed to know to become good wives and mothers. Abigail's mother taught Abigail and her two sisters how to cook, clean, sew, weave, make medicines from herbs, and raise vegetables. But Mrs. Smith taught Abigail something more.

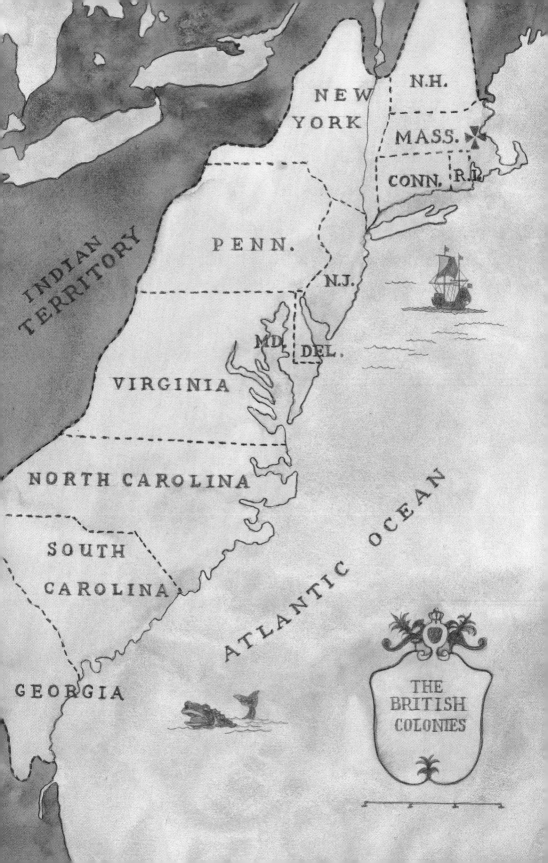

As the minister's wife, Mrs. Smith reached out to those who attended her husband's church. Abigail often went with Mrs. Smith when she cared for the sick and helped the elderly and the needy. Mrs. Smith's concern for others in the community made a great impression on young Abigail.

But her father's unusual views on women's education also had a great impact. Reverend Smith encouraged all three of his daughters, Mary, Abigail, and Elizabeth, to value education and to read to their hearts' content.

Abigail loved to sit by the fireplace and read the books from her father's home library. She delighted in them all, whether they were Greek myths, the poetry of Alexander Pope, or the plays of William Shakespeare.

Abigail also began writing letters to friends. She wrote of her thoughts, ideas, and wishes. It was a hobby that would last throughout her lifetime.

Mrs. Smith worried that Abigail's strong desire to learn was not a good thing. She felt that Abigail was far too stubborn and outspoken in her opinions. Those qualities were not thought to be ladylike. Luckily for Abigail, her father and grandmother defended her bright mind and her independent streak. Her grandmother often said, "Wild colts make the best horses."

CHAPTER 2
ABIGAIL'S BEST FRIEND

Abigail was a beautiful, slender, fair-skinned young woman. Her strong opinions, her love for learning, and her curiosity did not stop young men from being attracted to her. One was a young lawyer, John Adams. He was ten years older than Abigail and came from nearby Braintree. Short, stout John Adams was a friend of Mary, Abigail's older sister.

Slowly, after several years and many visits to the Smith home, John and Abigail realized that they were very much alike. They both had keen minds, firm views, and enjoyed sharing their ideas. Abigail and John became best friends and fell deeply in love.

On October 25, 1764, just weeks before her twentieth birthday, Abigail Smith married John Adams. They moved to his farm in nearby Braintree. For the first year of their marriage, life was just as Abigail might have expected. She cared for her new home and husband. She bade him good-bye when he rode off on horseback to the Boston law courts. She visited her family in Weymouth when the roads were not snow covered or mud filled. She kept up her passion for reading when time allowed, and she kept up her letter writing to friends.

In July of 1765, Abigail and John's first child was born. She was named Abigail, but called Nabby.

Abigail and John spent many
evenings by the fire, discussing the
latest news—the growing bad feeling
between the colonists and Britain.

Far from their cottage, across the Atlantic Ocean, the British king George III had finished fighting the seven-year French and Indian War. King George III began looking to the colonies for ways to replace the money he'd spent on that war.

In 1765 the British government created the Stamp Act. It stated that a stamp had to be purchased for all materials and documents printed in the colonies. That included all newspapers, marriage licenses, death certificates, deeds for buying and selling property, and even decks of playing cards.

The Stamp Act was a tax. The money collected from the stamps went back to Britain and gave no benefit to the colonies.

The chain of events caused by this Stamp Act changed the lives of Abigail and John Adams.

CHAPTER 3
TAXES! TAXES! TAXES!

Lawyers like John Adams were especially outraged by the Stamp Act. They couldn't do business without buying those stamps. The courts were shut down. Law offices, including John's, closed. But Abigail and John were not silent. They discussed how to oppose the actions of the king.

John began spending more and more time away from home. He met with other colonists, among them John Hancock, Benjamin Franklin, and his cousin Sam Adams. They urged people to ignore the Stamp Act.

Abigail didn't mind John's absences. She saw that their larger community— the Massachusetts colony—needed John's help.

One year after it was enacted, the Stamp Act was repealed. But stricter laws took its place.

In 1773, Britain passed the Tea Act. That law continued to tax the tea coming to the colonies, but from then on the colonists could buy their tea only from the company and merchants chosen by the British.

When three ships carrying tea sailed into Boston Harbor, Abigail, John, and many other colonists didn't want them to unload. That way no taxes would be due. But the British insisted on payment whether the tea was unloaded or not.

Angry colonists planned a way to protest. On the night of December 16, 1773, men dressed as Mohawks crept onto the ships and dumped the crates of tea into Boston Harbor.

Abigail and John thought that event, called the Boston Tea Party, was necessary. Britain had to see how furious the colonists were about being taxed without having a say in the matter.

Several months after the Boston Tea Party, John came to Abigail with exciting news. John, Ben Franklin, and others had been chosen to be part of a new group called the Continental Congress. It included men from all thirteen colonies. They would meet in Philadelphia to work out peaceful agreements with Britain on the things that were angering the colonists.

John would be far from home now, and stay away for longer periods of time. Besides their first child, Nabby, Abigail and John had three more children: John Quincy, Charles, and Thomas. (Their daughter Susanna died in 1770 at the age of two.) But Abigail saw that their much larger community—the thirteen colonies— needed John's help.

CHAPTER 4
WAR!

By the spring of 1775, John had been in Philadelphia for nine months. Abigail, like other colonists, feared war between the colonies and Britain would start at any moment. She missed John all the more.

Then, in April, Abigail heard the news. The war had begun with a battle at Lexington and Concord. The British soldiers, or redcoats, snuck toward Lexington hoping to attack. But Paul Revere and William Dawes warned the colonists ahead of time. The redcoats faced the Minutemen of Massachusetts.

War had broken out at Lexington and Concord. Then, on June 17, in Braintree, Abigail heard cannons firing and saw smoke billowing from Boston. It was the battle of Bunker Hill. She wrote John that with ". . . the constant roar of the cannon . . . we can not Eat, Drink or Sleep."

But that letter took a while to reach John. Like all mail, it traveled only as fast as a person on horseback could go. And Abigail couldn't count on John's letters to arrive in time to help her make family decisions. More and more, Abigail had to trust her own judgment.

She chose where and how to educate her children. She clung to her belief in equal education for boys and girls. So daughter Nabby learned Latin alongside her brothers. Abigail made decisions about the family money and who to hire to help with their farm. And she decided to buy nearby pieces of land when they came up for sale.

Her letters to John, filled with family news, eased his homesickness. They also offered strong opinions, especially her wishes for a stronger women's role in their new country. In March of 1776, she wrote, "I desire you would Remember the Ladies. . . . Do not put such unlimited power into the hands of the Husbands."

Through her letters she became John's eyes and ears. They were filled with what she had seen and heard at home. They gave John the fuel he needed to change the views of some Congress members. Some thought the fights in and around Boston were the work of a few "troublemakers." Her letters proved otherwise. John even quoted from one in a speech he gave.

Finally the representatives of the Continental Congress agreed. All thirteen colonies decided to break from British rule. On July 4, 1776, the group approved a document called the Declaration of Independence. And like her beloved country, Abigail was showing her own growing independence as well.

CHAPTER 5
ACROSS THE SEA

Throughout 1777, General George Washington and others won major battles. France joined with the colonists to fight the British.

That good news brought Abigail heartbreaking news as well. John had been asked to sail to France to join Benjamin Franklin there.

Their job was to convince France to trade directly with the colonists. She hated having John so far away, but Abigail saw that their much larger community—America—needed John's help. And Abigail made another sacrifice: She asked that their son John Quincy go to France too. Learning French and traveling would be an excellent education for him.

Abigail and the rest of her children couldn't join John and John Quincy. They didn't have the money. Abigail couldn't leave the farm unattended. And storms, and attacking British ships, made sea travel dangerous.

On February 13, 1778, a sad and worried Abigail said good-bye to John and ten-year-old John Quincy.

Once again Abigail was determined to be John's hands, eyes, and ears. She worked the farm. She cared for their family. And she wrote him long letters with news of home.

John and John Quincy returned home after a year and a half. But John was soon sent back to France, this time as head of the American group. Abigail agreed that their younger son Charles should travel to France with John and John Quincy. The three left in November of 1779.

By now, after being married for fifteen years, Abigail knew that John would spend his life in politics. She also knew that politicians didn't make much money. So Abigail found ways to plan for their later years. She had John send her goods from France, like silk hankies and fine glassware, which she sold. She put some of their money into businesses, and she bought and sold land. All the while, she cared for their family and farm.

In France, John was helping write the peace treaty between America and Britain. By January of 1784 all sides agreed that the American Revolutionary War was over.

Finally, after five long years away from John, forty-year-old Abigail, along with eighteen-year-old Nabby, crossed the Atlantic Ocean.

By August of 1784, Abigail and John were together once more. Home was not a cottage in Braintree. It was a thirty-room mansion in Paris, France, that John had rented. After one year there, John got exciting news. He'd been chosen as the first American ambassador to Britain.

In June of 1785, almost nine years after America declared war against King George III, Abigail was to meet that very same king.

Meeting King George III was just one of Abigail's pleasures in Britain. She also enjoyed seeing the plays of Shakespeare—the very ones she'd read as a girl.

CHAPTER 6
JOHN'S FIRST LADY

By 1788, after four years away, Abigail felt it was time to come home. She missed her grown children and little grandchildren. She wrote, ". . . I do not regret that I made this excursion since it has only more attached me to America."

Soon after they landed in Boston, a new government document took effect. It was the United States Constitution and called for a president and vice president.

George Washington was elected president and John Adams was elected vice president.

Once again Abigail saw that the far greater community—the United States of America—needed John's help. Once more she left Braintree and moved with John to the nation's first capital, New York City.

When George Washington's second term ended, John Adams was elected president. He was sworn in on March 4, 1797, in the nation's new capital, Philadelphia. Abigail, the new "First Lady," was in Braintree, caring for John's dying mother. John wrote her, "I never wanted your Advice and assistance more in my Life." Finally, in April, she joined John.

During his presidency the capital moved again, to an area named for George Washington.

John and Abigail moved into the still-unfinished President's House, known today as the White House. Abigail had to hang her laundry inside the house, since the grounds were muddy fields, like the rest of Washington, D.C.

John served for only one term. In 1801, they went home to Massachusetts for good.

Abigail cared for her family, her grandchildren, her garden, and of course, John. She saw their oldest son, John Quincy, follow in his father's political footsteps. But she never saw him take the oath of office as the sixth president of the United States. Abigail Adams died at home on October 28, 1818. She was almost seventy-four.

Abigail Adams was swept into the political events of the day. During her life she was guided by three loves: her love for learning, her love for her family, and her love for her country. Those—along with her greatest love, John Adams—helped her to shape the early history of the United States.

Abigail Adams Time Line

1744	Abigail is born on November 11 in Weymouth, Massachusetts.
1764	Abigail marries John on October 25.
1765	First child, Abigail, or "Nabby," is born on July 14.
1767	First son, John Quincy, is born on July 11.
1770	Second daughter, Susanna, dies at age two.
	Second son, Charles, is born on May 29.
1772	Third son, Thomas, is born on September 15.
1774	Abigail sees John off to Philadelphia for the Continental Congress.
1775	Abigail is alone with the children when the Revolutionary War starts on April 19.
1778	John and John Quincy sail for France in February.
1779	John and John Quincy return in August. They sail off again with Charles in November.
1782	Abigail welcomes Charles home in January.
1784	With the Revolutionary War now officially over, Abigail and Nabby sail for France on June 20.
1785–1787	Abigail and John, now first American ambassador to Britain, live in London.
1788	Abigail and John return to Boston on June 17.
1789	John is elected the country's first vice president.
1797	Abigail becomes First Lady in March after John is elected president.
1801	Abigail and John return to private life in March.
1818	Abigail dies at home on October 28.